TOM HENRICKSEN

Coding JavaScript

Along with an introduction to HTML and CSS

Contents

IV   Advanced JavaScript

Preface

As a developer, I thought I knew enough of HTML and CSS. I was wrong. I had to come back to the basics again and again. That is why I put this together. Plus I feel like JavaScript should be here too.

First, we start with some basics of HTML. You may have seen some of this before, but I find a review helpful. Then we cover some HTML5 changes. We touch on some of the major changes. Then we wrap up HTML with a discussion of tables, divs, and spans. These have confused me more than once...

The second section is devoted to CSS. This helps class things up a bit. We cover CSS basics, the box model, and CSS3. Similar to HTML5 it has some interesting updates.

The third part focuses on JavaScript basics. Covering topics like variables, functions, and conditionals. We also cover loops and closures too. In this quick start guide, we just focus on what you need to start working.

I

HTML

In part one, we start with the basics of HTML. We review the basics of HTML, HTML5, and divs and spans.

1

Targeted HTML Basics For Reliable People

Photo by Jackson Sophat on Unsplash

The web is created with some foundational technologies. Every website uses HTML or Hypertext Markup Language. It makes the content we consume online.

HTML

It gives structure to the pages we see. We can add images and links to a website with a series of elements and tags. Let's look at a simple example to get started.

```
<!DOCTYPE html>
<html>
<body>

<h1>Heading</h1>
<p>Paragraph.</p>

</body>
</html>
```

We start with the DOCTYPE to declare this is HTML. Then we have the open tag for HTML. As you look at the bottom you see the closing tag for HTML too. The body has similar tags to open and close the element.

Heading

We have a heading in our previous example. HTML Headings can be from <h1> to <h6>. It starts large and gets smaller as the number gets bigger.

```
<h1>Heading</h1>
<h2>Heading</h2>
<h3>Heading</h3>
<h4>Heading</h4>
<h5>Heading</h5>
<h6>Heading</h6>
```

If we open this in Chrome this is what you will see.

Heading

Heading

Heading

Heading

Heading

Heading

Paragraph

You can use the HTML paragraphs tag when you have a text block. We saw that in our first example. Here is another one.

```
<p>Lorem ipsum dolor sit amet, consectetur adipiscing elit,
sed do eiusmod tempor incididunt ut labore et dolore magna aliqua.</p>
```

Now these two are nice elements but the reason the web is powerful is links. Let's look at those next.

Link

The Hyperlink or link in HTML is the secret sauce. We can link to the document source or a reference.

```
<a href="https://codeiseasy.co">Code Is Easy</a>
```

Of course, sometimes we like to see a picture or image on the screen. To do this we need the image tag.

Image

The image tag helps us add visual components along with the text.

```
<img src="tom.jpg" alt="Tom Headshot" width="100"
height="150">
```

I added the width and height but these are not required. Although, it can help to keep the sizing correct.

Lists

HTML gives us two options for lists. Ordered and unordered lists.

```
<h2>Ordered List</h2>
<ol>
  <li>Apples</li>
  <li>Berries</li>
  <li>Currants</li>
</ol>

<h2>Unordered List</h2>
<ul>
  <li>Carrots</li>
  <li>Celery</li>
  <li>Onions</li>
</ul>
```

It looks like this if you open the file in a browser.

Ordered List

1. Apples
2. Berries
3. Currants

Unordered List

- Carrots
- Celery
- Onions

List examples

We covered some basics here for HTML. There is a lot more to learn. Of course, depending on your work this may be all you need. My development work has required me to use HTML periodically. Although, I am no expert. Play around with these and you will learn it well.

2

Important HTML5 Changes that Scream Out for Use

Photo by Jackson Sophat on Unsplash

HTML is like everything else. There are different versions we can use. HTML5 is a current version that has new features. Let's go through some of the changes and additions.

What is different?

Work has been done to remove the overlap between HTML, CSS, and JavaScript. Improvements have also been made to increase the readability of the code. Cross-browser consistency and responsiveness have been enhanced too. Finally, support of multimedia without plugins is another major change.

New Elements

In HTML5 there are new elements. The section tag was added to help organize the document.

```
<section>
<h2>Heading</h2>
<p>Lorem ipsum dolor sit amet, consectetur adipiscing
elit, sed do eiusmod tempor incididunt ut labore et
dolore magna aliqua. Ut enim ad minim veniam, quis
nostrud exercitation ullamco laboris nisi ut aliquip
ex ea commodo consequat. Duis aute irure dolor in
reprehenderit in voluptate velit esse cillum dolore
eu fugiat nulla pariatur. Excepteur sint occaecat
cupidatat non proident, sunt in culpa qui officia
deserunt mollit anim id est laborum.</p>
</section>
```

Similar to this tag we can also use header and footer tags. They are effectively organizing large chunks of HTML to make them more readable.

Form

To enable easier form creation HTML5 has added a few things.
Let's show the datetime-local input form element.

```
<input type="datetime-local">
```

If we run this in the browser we see this.

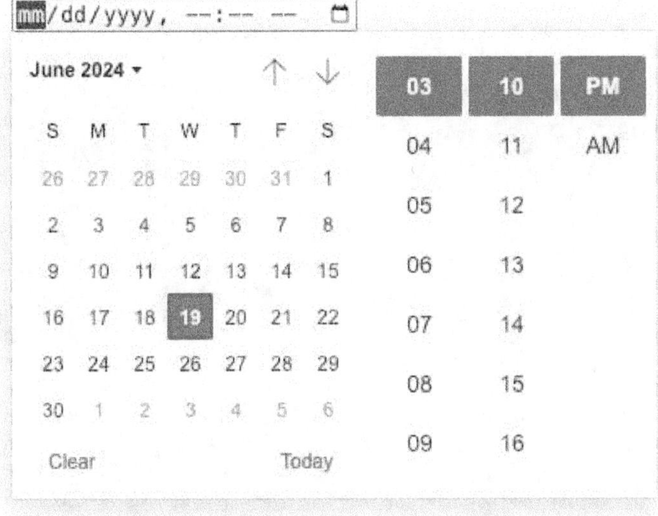

DateTime-Local example

That is nice compared to what we used to have to do for something like this.

Graphics

We can also add SVG or Scalable Vector Graphics in HTML5. Here is a simple example.

```
<svg width="100" height="100">
  <circle cx="50" cy="50" r="40" stroke="blue"
  stroke-width="4" fill="red" />
</svg>
```

If we run that in the browser you will see something like this.

SVG example

Not that impressive but it could be useful in some situations.

Offline

HTML5 enables offline work by storing local copies. So your browser will download the HTML, CSS, and JavaScript needed. This will allow you to work some without an internet connection.

HTML5 is a group of changes that enable better use of the web. From new elements and graphics, it helps the web take a step forward. Along with this, it makes the web more accessible. It is giving more and more people the ability to collaborate.

3

Practical HTML Tables, Divs, And Spans Make You Better

Photo by Alvin Engler on Unsplash

As I have worked with front-end technologies I see the approved way of working change. Web design norms come and go. HTML enables us various ways to create an interface.

Table

The HTML table is often derided but it can work. Early in my career tables were the way to go. Here is an example we can show the basic syntax.

```
<!DOCTYPE html>
<html>
    <style>
        table, th, td {
          border:1px solid black;
        }
        </style>
<body>

<table>
  <tr>
    <th>Company</th>
    <th>State</th>
    <th>Employees</th>
  </tr>
  <tr>
    <td>Balloons Inc.</td>
    <td>Ohio</td>
    <td>250</td>
  </tr>
  <tr>
    <td>Cement Co.</td>
    <td>Arizona</td>
    <td>4510</td>
  </tr>
</table>
```

```
</body>
</html>
```

Running this code gives us a simple table to display our data. Plan to not be amazed!

Company	State	Employees
Balloons Inc.	Ohio	250
Cement Co.	Arizona	4510

HTML Table Example

This simple example gives you an idea of how to use tables. There is a lot more we can do with them depending on your requirements.

Div

The div element is short for division. It creates a **block-level** section of HTML. We can style the div with CSS and manipulate it with JavaScript.

```
<!DOCTYPE html>
<html>
<head>
<style>
.exampleDiv {
  background-color: lightblue;
}
</style>
</head>
<body>

<h1>Let's talk about div elements!</h1>

<div class="exampleDiv">
  <h2>h2 in a div element</h2>
  <p>Text in a div element.</p>
</div>

<p>We have broken out of the div.</p>

</body>
</html>
```

We have an example that has the div in light blue. That way you can see where the div starts and stops.

Let's talk about div elements!

h2 in a div element

Text in a div element.

We have broken out of the div.

Div element example

In the picture, you can see the boundaries of the div and the rest of the page. If we applied styling it would only be within the div element.

Span

A span is an **inline container** we can add to an HTML document. Where a div is block-level and the span is inline. These are differences you may want to remember.

```
<!DOCTYPE html>
<html>
<body>

<h1>HTML Span element</h1>

<p>The fire truck is <span
style="color:red;font-weight:bold">red</span>.</p>
```

```
<p>The tree is <span
style="color:green;font-weight:bold">green</span>.</p>

</body>
</html>
```

Here we have two span elements used. We apply the styling here to change the color and put the font in bold.

HTML Span element

The fire truck is red.

The tree is **green**.

HTML Span example

We can see that the code does here. The next time you need a container for your HTML you can explore all three. The table, div, and span each have their pros and cons. Try out a simple example first to see what fits the bill correctly.

II

CSS

CSS is quite helpful in making websites more appealing. I have overlooked this for too long. I review some basics and then cover the box model. Finally, we cover CSS3.

4

The Truth About CSS Will Make You Something

Photo by Marcus Ganahl on Unsplash

Have you ever seen a website that looked weird? Do the fonts need to be corrected? This is when the CSS didn't load. It essentially makes the web look nice. I am not a font person but I understand the need for style.

CSS

CSS or Cascading Style Sheets apply the styling to websites. From text size and fonts, it can bring a touch of class to things.

```
<!DOCTYPE html>
<html>
<head>
<style>
body {
   background-color: lightpink;
}

h1 {
   color: white;
   text-align: center;
}

p {
   font-family: verdana;
   font-size: 20px;
}
</style>
</head>
<body>

<h1>H1 Heading(with center align)</h1>
<p>Paragraph(font size 20px and font verdana.</p>

</body>
</html>
```

Here is a simple HTML file with styling added. In this, we apply a background color to the body of the HTML. Then to the H1 heading we change the color and center the text. For the paragraph, we change the font and size. It looks like this.

H1 Heading(with center align)

Paragraph(font size 20px and font verdana.

HTML with Internal CSS Example

While HTML was just meant for text CSS was created to add style. If you are old enough to remember the initial web you are thankful! Things have come a long way.

Ways to Include

We showed you an example of an internal CSS above. The style tag is added in the HTML. We could also create an external document to put our CSS in.

```
<!DOCTYPE html>
<html>
<head>
<link rel="stylesheet" href="external-style.css">
</head>
<body>
```

```
<h1>We are using a CSS from another file.</h1>
<p>Aren't you impressed!</p>

</body>
</html>
```

This is our HTML file. Next, we can show you the code for the external CSS file.

```css
body {
   background-color: lightblue;
}


h1 {
   color: navy;
   margin-left: 20px;
}
```

This works nicely as you can see below.

We are using a CSS from another file.

Aren't you impressed!

HTML with External CSS Example

With this example, you have two files. In a small example like this, it seems like overload. This is quite helpful in larger pages or if you have multiple pages. Then you can create one CSS file and include it in other HTML documents.

The last type is inline. See how the styling is in line here:

```html
<!DOCTYPE html>
<html>
  <head>
    <title>Inline CSS</title>
  </head>
  <body>
    <p style="color:rgb(149, 0, 255);font-size:46px;">
      I'm a big, purple, <strong>Proud UNI
      Panther</strong>!
    </p>
  </body>
</html>
```

This is mixing the CSS and HTML. For a beginner, this could be not very clear. Here is what it looks like.

I'm a big, purple, **Proud UNI Panther**!

HTML with Inline CSS Example

So when you add CSS to your HTML you have options on how to do it. As we discussed each way has its pros and cons. Depending on the size of your project and the team you are working with.

5

Wondrous CSS Box Model Made Instructive

Photo by Kelli McClintock on Unsplash

At first, CSS seemed like a black art for magicians only. Then as

I began to learn more it began to make sense. The box model is used to describe the design and layout of elements.

CSS Box Model

Each element has a box around it. Sometimes you can see it, other times it seems to disappear.

Content — what is in the box, text, or image
Padding — the area around the content, is transparent
Border - goes around the padding and content
Margin - the area outside of the border, it is also transparent
Here is an example.

```
<!DOCTYPE html>
<html>
<head>
<style>
div {
   background-color: lightgrey;
   width: 300px;
   border: 10px solid red;
   padding: 25px;
   margin: 20px;
}
</style>
</head>
<body>

<h2>CSS Box Model</h2>

<p>A box around each component.</p>

<div>The content.<br>
 25px padding<br>
```

```
20px margin<br>
10px red border.</div>

</body>
</html>
```

It looks like this.

CSS Box Model

A box around each component.

The content.
25px padding
20px margin
10px red border.

CSS Box Model Example

Size Math

To make the box the correct size we need to do some math. I know you weren't expecting that. It's easy so you won't be confused.

```
<!DOCTYPE html>
<html>
<head>
<style>
div {
   width: 300px;
   height: 65px;
   padding: 10px;
   border: 5px solid gray;
   margin: 0;
}
</style>
</head>
<body>

<h2>CSS Box Model Math</h2>

<div>This box is 300px wide and 50 px high. The
padding is 10px per side so 20px total. Then the
border 5px per side so 10px total. The total width of
this element is also 330px.</div>

</body>
</html>
```

When we run this code you will see the following.

CSS Box Model Math

This box is 300px wide and 50 px high. The padding is 10px per side so 20px total. Then the border 5px per side so 10px total. The total width of this element is also 330px.

CSS Box Model Math Example

We must add the content, padding, and border to get the total width. After I learned this CSS made more sense. Before I would start changing things trying to make it look right.

6

How To Make CSS3 Scream Simplified

Photo by KOBU Agency on Unsplash

As the web has changed so has the technology that supports it. CSS3 is one of these examples. CSS was originally released in

1996. A few years later CSS3 was released in 2005.

Benefits

One of the main benefits of CSS3 is responsive web design. It replaces clunky sites with more streamlined performance. There are new advanced animations and opacity features in CSS3.

Another benefit is the ability to break pages into modules. Media queries are also a new thing in CSS3. Plus we can now apply gradients and rounded corners as well.

Example

Let's look at an example of linear gradients.

```html
<!DOCTYPE html>
<html lang="en">
<head>
<meta charset="utf-8">
<title>CSS Example of Linear Gradients from Top to
Bottom</title>
<style>
  .gradient {
  width: 400px;
  height: 300px;
  /* Fallback for browsers that don't support
  gradients */
  background: red;
  /* For Safari 5.1 to 6.0 */
  background: -webkit-linear-gradient(red, yellow);
  /* For Internet Explorer 10 */
  background: -ms-linear-gradient(red, yellow);
  /* Standard syntax */
  background: linear-gradient(red, yellow);
```

```
  }
</style>
</head>
<body>
    <div class="gradient"></div>
</body>
</html>
```

When we look at this in the browser.

CSS3 Linear Gradient Example

What else can CSS3 do?

Box Shadow

It can also allow you to create a box shadow. Let's take a look.

```html
<!DOCTYPE html>
<html lang="en">
<head>
<meta charset="utf-8">
<title>Example of CSS3 Box Shadow Effect</title>
<style>
    .box{
  width: 200px;
  height: 150px;
  background: #ccc;
  box-shadow: 5px 5px 10px #999;
 }
</style>
</head>
<body>
    <div class="box"></div>
</body>
</html>
```

Open that in your browser and you should see something like this.

CSS3 Box Shadow Example

CSS3 has brought some major updates to CSS. As the web evolves there will be new updates. As a person who loves learning it is exciting to see the changes in the web. It is becoming easier to use and more robust.

III

JavaScript

In part three, we start with the basics of JavaScript. We code some fundamental aspects to help you understand how to get around.

7

JavaScript A Useful Tool For Tired Minds

I have a confession. JavaScript and I started badly. My first foray was for form validation. I would cuss about its existence.

As luck would have after being reintroduced to it I began to respect it. Over the years it has grown into a powerful language.

JavaScript

With its humble beginnings, JavaScript has evolved into a modern programming language. From the browser to the server it can handle almost everything. Node.js gives it a powerful framework on the server side.

Mozilla created it and here is how they define it. "JavaScript is a lightweight interpreted programming language with first-class functions." That is a mouthful!

Code

Let's look at some basic code. It is an HTML file displaying some JavaScript. Save this code to your local machine.

```
<!DOCTYPE html>

<head>
    <title>JavaScript example code</title>
    <style>

    </style>
</head>
<body>
    <script>
    alert("JavaScript is working!")
    </script>
    <h1>Test 1</h1>
    <h2>Test 2</h2>
    Regular text
</body>
```

When we run this we will see this.

JavaScript alert message

Once you click ok you will see this.

Test 1

Test 2

Regular text

HTML Screen-shot

Statement

The statement is the basic instruction for JavaScript. We can create some variables and then assign them values.

```
let a, b, c;      // Statement creating three variables
a = 2;            // Statement assign the value of 2 to
```

```
variable a
b = 3;            // Statement assign the value of 3 to
variable b
c = a + b;        // Statement assign a plus b to c
```

The **semicolon** is at the end of the statement. However, we could put multiple statements together.

```
a = 2; b = 3;
```

This isn't as readable so most programmers prefer not to. So just because you can do something doesn't mean you should.

Functions

When we want to perform a task we can create a function. If we need to sum two numbers we could do this in code or create a function.

```
// Add two numbers
num3 = num1 + num2;


// Function to sum two numbers
function sumTwoNumbers(num1, num2) {
  return num1 + num2;
}
```

In this example, we perform the same code one in a function and one not. Using a function has value. We can call it repeatedly. Also, we could easily add some error checking too.

```javascript
// Function to sum two numbers
function sumTwoNumbers(num1, num2) {
   return num1 + num2;
}


let sum = sumTwoNumbers(6,4);
```

We can do it like this example if you want to call the function. Here we pass in two numbers. These numbers could be replaced with variables as well.

In closing, we have touched on why we would use JavaScript. Then we started to code. Using statements and functions we began to see what is under the hood. Try it out for yourself! You won't regret it.

8

Look I found these astounding benefits of JavaScript variables and values

9

First easy JavaScript function basics that are the most fascinating

Photo by Stanley Dai on Unsplash

Functions are the powerhouse in JavaScript. This is where the work happens. Do we need to calculate the space of a floor? This calls for a function.

```
function calculateFlooring(length, width) {
  return length * width;
}
```

This function will calculate the flooring we need if we remodel the kitchen. So why do we need functions?

Benefits

Think of a function as a container for your code. Similar to a code block but, we can call this function repeatedly. This will facilitate reusable code.

In our prior example, you could copy the statement. Of course, if we wanted to change that we needed to search for that code and change all the occurrences.

Example

In our first function example, we calculated the flooring. Let's step back and make it even easier. We can print something on the screen.

```
function greetTom() {
  alert("Hello Tom!");
}
```

Of course, you can put your name in place of mine. If you want to keep the tradition, you can replace it with "Hello World". Have you wondered why that is the tradition, look here.

Calling

The code may look nice but nothing happens if you don't call it. How do you do that? I am glad you asked. Here is an example.

```
function greetTom() {
  alert("Hello Tom!");
}


greetTom();
// do other things...
```

That call is easy as it takes no arguments. In our first function, we had two arguments we needed. Let's try that next.

Passing arguments

In our first example, we started with a function to calculate flooring. It took two arguments.

```
function calculateFlooring(length, width) {
  return length * width;
}

calculateFlooring(12,10);
```

We can pass in the two numbers to get the flooring needed. In this example, we hard-code the value. You won't do that often or ever.

```
function calculateFlooring(length, width) {
  return length * width;
}


calculateFlooring(length,width);
```

As you see here, we have the two arguments as variables. The names are the same as the function but don't have to be.

Returning data

It is helpful when we return the calculation. If we don't the function is not as useful as it could be. We just need to use the return. We did this in our calculate flooring function. Although we need to assign this or print it out.

```
function calculateFlooring(length, width) {
  return length * width;
}


let totalFlooring = 0;
totalFlooring = calculateFlooring(length,width);
```

Now we can use this value later in the application. The prior examples didn't use the value returned. This is always an option if you don't need it later on.

Functions can do a lot for us. They provide us with a container for our code. Then we can call them and pass parameters. Along with that, they can return the data. If you need more information here is some further reading.

10

Avoid painful mistakes with these Simplistic JavaScript Conditionals

Photo by Artur Aldyrkhanov on Unsplash

Applications help us make decisions. A basic decision is an if condition. For example, if the pizza delivery driver arrives open the door. JavaScript like other languages has many conditionals like Java.

if

An if statement starts with a condition. If it is true the statement following will happen.

```
if(pizzaArrives) {
  openTheDoor();
}
```

So if pizzaArrives is true we call the function openTheDoor. I added the braces after the if statement. This is optional but helps readability. Omitting the braces can cause you to miss bugs. So please include them!

if/else

There are times when you have two different courses of action. We can add the else statement along with the if. Say you are cooking some hamburgers.

```
if(sideCooked) {
  flipBurger();
} else {
  keepCooking();
}
```

This check can run the cooking robot at your favorite house of burgers. It might need some more code though.

If you need to check two conditions you can have an if else if too.

```
if(sideCooked) {
  flipBurger();
} else if(otherSideCooked) {
  removeFromGrill();
} else {
  keepCooking();
}
```

This gives us the option to check additional values. If you need more checks a switch statement may work better. More on that later.

Conditional Operators

The operators we use for if statements must resolve to true or false. There are quite a few options for you to use here. Speaking from experience you need to test things out and get the right one.

```
if(9>5) { alert("Greater than"); }// greater than
if(5<8) { alert("Less than"); } // less than
if(9>=6) { alert("Greater than equal to"); } //
greater than equal to
if(4<=6) { alert("Less than equal to"); } // less
than equal to
if(4!=6) { alert("Not equal to"); } // not equal to
```

There are also two logical operators. The Logical And(&&) and the Logical Or(||). They are used a lot but don't be intimidated.

```
const value1 = 4;
const value2= -3;

console.log(value1 > 0 && value2 > 0); // Expected
output: false
console.log(value1 > 0 || value2 > 0); // Expected
output: true
```

The Logical And must have both values true to resolve as true. The Logical Or needs one to be true.

switch

Switch statements evaluate the expression to determine which statement to execute. Then it runs the code until reaching a break statement. Here is an example that tells us the price of the shoes you want.

```
const shoes = 'Reebok';
switch (shoes) {
  case 'Nike':
    console.log('Nike shoes are $200.');
    break;
  case 'Adidas':
  case 'Reebok':
    console.log('Adidas and Reebok are $100 a pair.');
    // Expected output: "Adidas and Reebok are $100 a
    pair."
    break;
  default:
```

```javascript
    console.log(`Sorry, we don't carry ${shoes}.`);
  }
```

This code should print "Adidas and Reebok are $100 a pair." to the console. Switch statements can be tricky if you don't add the break statement.

```javascript
const shoes = 'Nike';
switch (shoes) {
  case 'Nike':
    console.log('Nike shoes are $200.');
  case 'Adidas':
  case 'Reebok':
    console.log('Adidas and Reebok are $100 a pair.');
    break;
  default:
    console.log(`Sorry, we don't carry ${shoes}.`);
}
```

In this example, we removed the break from the Nike statement. Do you know what happens here? It will print 'Nike shoes are $200.' and then 'Adidas and Reebok are $100 a pair.' This type of bug is common for beginner programmers. Don't feel bad. You are now part of the club!

Conditionals are fundamental to JavaScript. Similar to other languages it allows us to provide solutions quickly. The if/else and switch are easy to use.

11

JavaScript has Sizable loops that will explode your mind

Photo by Kier in Sight Archives on Unsplash

As a kid, we planted a windbreak on our farm. A line of trees that needed watering a few times a week. Turn on the hose water the first tree and count to ten. Move to the second tree and repeat.

Similar to life our computer programs must repeat things. That's where loops come in handy. For loops are quite common so let's start there.

for

If we have an array of books and we would like to print them out. We could use the following loop.

```
for (let i = 0; i < books.length; i++) {
  text += books[i] + "<br>";
}
```

The for loop has three basic parts. Start, Condition, and Step.

start

This is the part where we set up the loop variable. In our example that is **i**. Usually, we initialize to zero. Although, you can set it to say 10 and then count down too.

condition

Next is the condition where check to see if we need to run this loop again. Our example checks if we still have more books to loop through. If we are done we stop.

step

The last part is the step. This tells us what happens after each iteration. Our example uses the increment operator(++). This is the normal step but we can do other things for special cases.

while

If my dog Baxter wants to eat I want to create a loop that feeds him while he is hungry. The while loop can do this. Here is an example.

```
let baxterHungry = true;

while (baxterHungry) {
    console.log(feedBaxter);
    checKBaxter();
}
```

We set the variable to true. Then we feed the dog until it becomes false. The while loop evaluates the condition we give it. It needs to resolve to be true or false.

If it is true the code inside the loop executes. We evaluate the condition again. Once the condition becomes false the loop stops.

do-while

The for and while loops check the condition then run the code statements. The do-while is different in that it runs the code and then checks your condition. It is less common but useful in special situations.

```javascript
let donutsEaten = 0;
do {
   console.log("Donuts eaten " + donutsEaten);
   donutsEaten++;
} while (donutsEaten < 5)
console.log("I'm full of Donuts!");
```

The do while runs until the condition is false—Opposite of the two other types of loops we have discussed. The output would look like this.

```
Donuts eaten 0
Donuts eaten 1
Donuts eaten 2
Donuts eaten 3
Donuts eaten 4
I'm full of Donuts!
```

When you need to loop through code JavaScript has a few options for you. Like other programming languages, it has the for, while, and do-while loops. Just make sure it fits your needs.

12

Surprisingly Improved JavaScript Variable Scope You Need

Photo by Markus Spiske on Unsplash

My wife changes topics quickly. I joke with her that she needs turn signals. That way I can keep up with the shifting focus. She is talking about dinner, and then we shift to our next vacation.

Scope

Our code has a similar concept with scope. Variables can come in and out of scope quickly. As developers, we must keep this concept front and center.

In JavaScript, they have a few different types of scope. We can use them accordingly. If you have done other coding you have encountered similar concepts.

Global

Global scope items are visible everywhere. In our example, we create a visible variable in the function and outside.

```
let myGlobalVariable = "TheBigGlobalVariable";

function logOutGlobalVariable() {
    console.log(myGlobalVariable);
}

logOutGlobalVariable();
```

I bet you are wondering, what if I add a variable in the function? This leads us to the local scope example.

Local

Local variables are visible only in the function. Here is an example to try this out.

```
let myGlobalVariable = "TheBigGlobalVariable";

function logOutGlobalVariable() {
    console.log(myGlobalVariable);
    let localVariable = "TheLocalOne";
    console.log(localVariable);
}

logOutGlobalVariable();

console.log(localVariable);
```

If we run this we will get an error on the last line.

```
console.log(localVariable);
            ^

ReferenceError: localVariable is not defined
```

So you can see what happens when you mistakenly place a variable in the wrong spot.

Block

Where local scope is within the function, block scope is within the braces. Sometimes you create braces to identify some code. Let's take a look to show you what I mean.

```javascript
console.log("here");
{
  let blockScopeVariable = 0;
  console.log(blockScopeVariable);
}
// we can't reference blockScopeVariable here
console.log(blockScopeVariable); // won't work
```

As you can see we create a block scope variable within the braces. Then outside of that, it won't be able to be referenced.

Gotchas

The scope can be confusing and lead to some errors. As you get more experience with JavaScript, you can spot them early on. For instance, if we look at this code snippet:

```javascript
const colors = ['red', 'blue', 'white'];

for (let i = 0, var l = colors.length; i < l; i++) {
  console.log(colors[i]); // 'red', 'blue', 'white'
}
console.log(l); // ???
console.log(i); // ???
```

The variables i and l will get reference errors. They are out of scope similar to our previous examples. Dmitri Pavlutin explains this more in-depth here. He also covers a few more common mistakes we may make in coding.

JavaScript scope has a few basic principles you need to remember. Global scope is visible everywhere. Local and Block scope are more focused. Overall you should use the latter and avoid the former. Keep on coding!

13

Exploit JavaScript Closures More and Don't Panic

Photo by Cristina Gottardi on Unsplash

Having dipped into JavaScript occasionally over my development career Closures have been something I didn't encounter much. They have some great value.

Closures

How can we define closures? Well, this article defines it like this. "Closure in JavaScript is a form of **lexical scoping** used to preserve variables from the outer scope of a function in the inner scope of a function."

```
function outerFunction() {
  var x = 10;
  function innerFunction() {
    return x;
  }
  return innerFunction;
}

var inner = outerFunction();
console.log(inner());
```

Here is an example of a closure. The outer function outer-Function() creates a variable x and a function innerFunction(). The inner function innerFunction() returns the value of the variable x. The outer function then returns the inner function innerFunction().

Next inner function innerFunction() is then assigned to the variable inner. When the variable inner is called, it returns the value of the variable x, even though the outer function outerFunction() has already returned.

In a moment we can cover lexical scoping. First, let's understand why we need them. Plus some disadvantages too.

Pros and Cons

Closures can help hide the encapsulation details. Like Java's private variables and functions, this allows us to control access. The downside of this is closures take up more memory. These items can not be garbage collected. Lastly, it can slow down execution. Deepak Mankotia explores this more in-depth.

Lexical Scoping

The term lexical scoping refers to where the variable is defined. Along with that where it can be referenced or not.

```
let x = 10
let myFunc = function (){
let y = 20;
    console.log("x and y is accessible (outer):", x,
    y);
    let insideFunc= function (){
        let z = 30;
        console.log("x and y and z is accessible
        (inner):", x, y, z);
    }
    insideFunc();
    return;
}
myFunc();
console.log("only x is accessible (global):", a);
```

In this example, insideFunc is defined within the myFunc. In this case, myFunc is its parent. That of the parent function lexically binds the child function. JavaScript Closures are a form of Lexical Scoping.

JavaScript Closures are powerful tools. They have some distinct values. It allows you to encapsulate details but, it can slow down your execution time. Consider whether the risks and rewards work for your application.

For more information here is a deep dive on Closures.

IV

Advanced JavaScript

In this section, we get into the deep end of the pool. JavaScript objects and arrays can trip people up. So we spend time going over each. We finish talking about the spread and rest operator.

14

Unparalleled JavaScript Objects Make You Thrilled

Photo by Hari Krishnan on Unsplash

I used mostly procedural languages in my first few years of software development. Mostly PL/SQL was the language I used. Even the object-oriented work I did wasn't harnessing the full strength of the language.

JavaScript wasn't originally object-oriented. It has been modified to become more powerful. The changes particularly in

ECMAScript 6 were quite large.

Today we use objects in JavaScript all the time. As an old Java developer, I see the value that they bring. Although, this can be a big change for developers to understand.

What are they?

The JavaScript objects represent real things, such as my car from high school. Let's create it here with some of the properties.

```
// Create an object:
const car = {
 type:"Chevrolet",
 model:"Malibu",
    year:"1976",
    color:"red"
    };
```

JavaScript objects are one of the many data types allowed in the language. There are a few others as you can see. Although, in your development work you will primarily use primitives and objects.

Objects vs Primitive

In this article, they go in-depth on this. I just want to point out a few key differences. **Objects are mutable and primitive types are not.** Mutable means they can be changed.

```
// Create an object:
const car = {
```

```
  type:"Chevrolet",
  model:"Malibu",
     year:"1976",
     color:"red"
     };


 let ball = "basketball"; // primitive
```

Adding to our previous example, we have the car object and the ball primitive. The former can be changed while the latter cannot be. As an old Java programmer, this is quite familiar.

Constructor

Objects can be created using a constructor. Continuing with the car theme let's create two car objects so you can see what it looks like.

```
// Constructor function for Car objects
function Car(make, model, year) {
  this.make = make;
  this.model = model;
  this.year = year;
}

// Create two Car objects
const myCar = new Car("Ford", "Pinto", "1971");
const yourCar = new Car("Dodge", "Charger", "1977");
```

This works similarly to our previous example. We are using the function keyword here to designate the constructor. Also, we use the new keyword as well for the object creation.

Properties

We created two car objects with lots of values on them. These are called properties. If we want to print them out to the log we can do this.

```
console.log(myCar.make);
console.log(myCar.model);
```

This is one way to access the value. Or you can do it this way as well.

```
console.log(myCar["make"]);
console.log(myCar["model"];
```

So you have options to get at the underlying data. In my experience, the former is used more than the latter. Your mileage may vary.

Methods

JavaScript objects have some built-in methods. For instance, one is the keys() method. This converts the keys to an array.

```
// Initialize an object
const car = {
  make: 'Ford',
  model: 'Pinto',
  yeear: '1971'
};
```

```javascript
// Get the keys of the object
const keys = Object.keys(car);

console.log(keys);
// outputs the following
["make", "model", "yeear"]
```

There also is a values() method too.

```javascript
// Initialize an object
const game = {
    id: 1,
    date: `23-March-2025`,
    teams: 'Panthers vs Jayhawks',
    location: 'St. Louis'
};

// Get all values of the object
const values = Object.values(game);

console.log(values);
// outputs the following
[1, "23-March-2025", "Panthers vs Jayhawks", "St.
Louis"]
```

This can be helpful along with a loop to iterate through them. There are other methods too. This post reviews more built-in methods.

This

JavaScript has reserved this as a keyword. It is used to reference the current object. Here is what that can look like.

```javascript
// Create an object:
const car = {
  make: "Dodge",
  model: "Charger",
  year: "2015",
  carDetails : function() {
    return this.make + " " + this.model + " " +
    this.year;
  }
};
```

In this example, we create an object with three properties. When we want to display the details we can call the carDetails function. It would display "Dodge Charger 2015" in this case.

As a keyword, this cannot be used as a variable name. Also, we can't change the value that this refers to. This in JavaScript has three contexts: function, class, and global. We have shared the function context in these examples. There is more information here.

JavaScript objects are similar to other language objects. However, there are a few differences too. It is important to remember that JavaScript didn't start this way. It continues to change and adapt. If you know the basics you can use it well.

15

Easily Pluck Better JavaScript Arrays

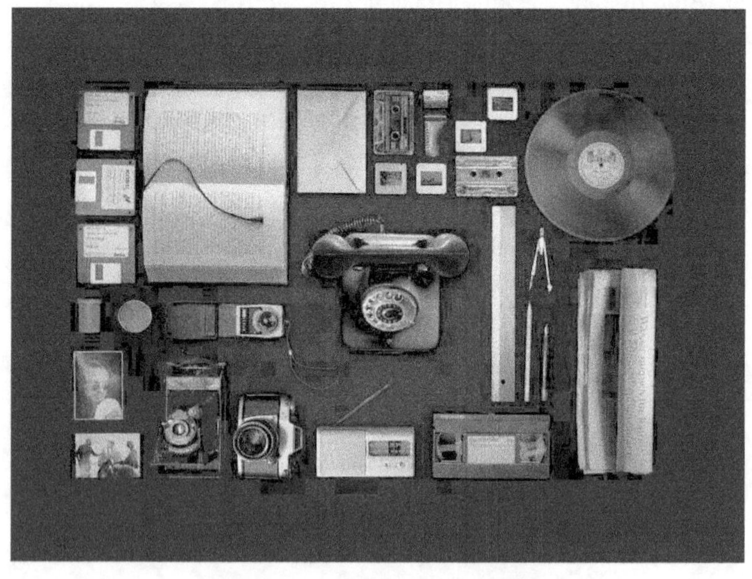

Photo by Julius Drost on Unsplash

My wife enjoys organizing things. She put them in envelopes

by year. JavaScript Arrays are similar to envelopes. We can put multiple objects in them.

JavaScript Arrays

JavaScript Arrays store multiple objects in one collection. They also provide some common operations. The collection can contain numerous data types such as strings, numbers, objects, or other arrays.

Create

There are a few ways to create an array in JavaScript.

```
const bread = ["white", "wheat", "sourdough"];
```

This is an array of bread. We set the values as we declare them.

```
const fruits = [];
fruits.push("banana", "apple", "peach");
```

This array is declared and then we push the fruits into the array.

```
const cars = new Array("Chevy", "Jaguar", "Porsche",
"Fiat");
```

The new keyword can be used as in this example.

```
let arrOfManyTypes = ['abc', 1, 2, 3, true, 'xyz'];
```

An array can also have multiple data types. My previous ones had similar data types but this one has strings, numbers, and a boolean.

Modify

We can modify arrays with built-in methods. The toString() can make it a string to print out.

```
const bread = ["white", "wheat", "sourdough"];

console.log(bread.toString()); //
white,wheat,sourdough
```

The join method will pull the elements together too similar to toString.

```
const bread = ["white", "wheat", "sourdough"];

console.log(bread.join('-')); // white-wheat-sourdough
```

The push method we used before can modify arrays.

```
const fruits = [];
fruits.push("banana", "apple", "peach");
```

The push method adds the elements at the end of the array. There are many more that you can see here.

Zero-based

I don't want you to miss out on that JavaScript Arrays are zero-based. Where some languages start at 1 JavaScript acts like Java in this regard.

```
let tomsArray = [11, 22, 33, 44, 55];
console.log(tomsArray[0]); // prints 11
```

In this example, if we want to get the value of 33 we need to pass in the value 2 to the array. This can cause bugs in your code so make sure you understand this.

Otherwise, getting an element is easy once you get past that fact. Use your square brackets and the correct index. Then you will be able to access any of the elements in the array.

So we have whetted your appetite for JavaScript Arrays. You know a little more than when you started. We talked about creating and modifying them. Plus we touched on how to access them and don't forget they are zero-based. Happy Coding!

16

Quick JavaScript Type Conversion and Coercion That Will Make Code Better

Photo by Austin Distel on Unsplash

As you work in code you see changes. Some of them require your manual intervention. While others the language will handle them for you. Starting with C, C++, then Java I saw these subtleties at work.

As we work with JavaScript we see similar changes. The two types we want to discuss here are Type Conversion and Type Coercion. They have some similarities. Let's review them and how they relate and differ.

Type Conversion

There can be times when we need to convert a number to a string and vice versa. Perhaps you need to process input from the user or another system. Type conversion in JavaScript is a manual process.

```
const inputYear = "1992";
console.log(Number(inputYear), inputYear); // 1992 "1992"
console.log(String(73), 73); // 73 73

console.log(Number("Tom")); // NaN
```

These are a few examples that we start with a string. Using the Number function we can explicitly change it. Likewise, we can use the String function to convert the number to a string. Note what happens when we try to convert my first name to a number.

Type Coercion

Have you ever done something and wondered, "Who did that?" That has happened to me. It's like I have an automatic drive that changes things I didn't realize.

JavaScript has Type Coercion that operates automatically. We have a few examples here to share. The first one takes the number 43 and makes it a string.

```
console.log('I am ' + 43 + ' years old'); // I am 43
years old
console.log(2 + 3 + 4 + '5'); // 95
console.log('10' - '4' - '3' - 2 + '5'); // 15
```

Next, we add a few numbers and then a string. Of course, JavaScript says, "I think Tom meant that as a number." Then it changes it for me. Finally, we reverse it by using subtraction on strings coerced to numbers.

Type coercion can introduce bugs if you don't understand it. This article can help you sort some of that out. Try out some examples to see it in action. Type Conversion and Coercion are different but useful. Handle with care.

17

Actually, JavaScript Has Surprising And Practical Strings

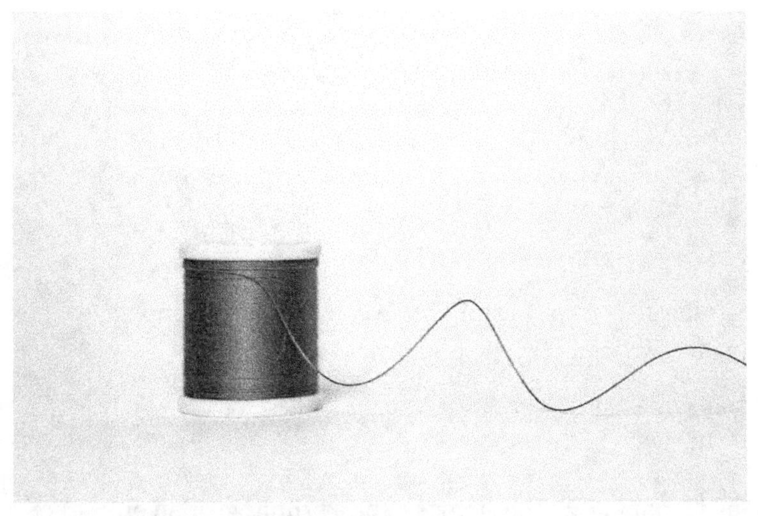

Photo by amirali mirhashemian on Unsplash

As a coder who writes I use a lot of words. When we want to create words in our JavaScript code we can use strings. From mundane text on our screen to personalize messages strings can work for us.

String

When we want to create a string we can do it just like this.

```
let myFirstString = "My First String";
```

There is a lot to learn about strings.

Create

As we did before we can create strings in a few different ways. Let's review some of the different ways.

```
let mySecondString = "My Second String";
let stringSingleQuite = 'Example using single quotes';
let backTicksToo = `We can use back ticks too`;
```

Similar to our first example we can use double quotes. Single quotes are legal as well as backticks too.

Primitive vs Objects

JavaScript allows the strings to be a primitive or an object.

```
let primitiveString = "This is a primitive";
let objectString = new String("This is an object.");
```

The first example is primitive and similar to our previous examples. The second is an object. We use the new keyword and the String constructor. If you would like to know more check out this post from Flavio.

functions

There are a myriad of functions that we can use on strings in JavaScript. We can look over a few.

length

We can get the length of the string with the length function.

```
let sampleText = "A long time ago in a galaxy far far
away...";
let length = sampleText.length;
```

This can be used a lot with loops.

indexOf

The indexOf can give us the location of a word or letter.

```
let sentence = "A quick brown fox jumped over the
lazy dog.";
let foxIndex = text.indexOf("fox");
```

Using the indexOf and the slice function can help you break strings apart.

slice

If you need to pull out parts of a string the slice function can come in handy.

```
let animals = "Fox, Horse, Cow";
let farmAnimals = animals.slice(5);
```

We take the last two words of this string and create a new string.

Comparing

Comparing strings in JavaScript has two types. Strict and loose comparisons that are subtly different.

```
let str1 = "IowaBasketball";
let str2 = "Basketball";

console.log(str1 === str2); // false
```

This is an example of strict comparison.

```
let num1= 23;
let num2 = '23';

// Loose Equality
console.log(num1 == num2); // true
// Strict Equality
console.log(num1 === num2); // false
```

Here we compare the two types. Where the loose equality works the strict does not. There is also the localCompare you can consider.

We have just scratched the surface here. I think we have given you a nice overview of JavaScript strings. From creating them to the functions we can use you know the lay of the land. For homework spend some time coding strings and filling in your understanding.

18

This Is What JavaScript Numbers Opportunities Make

Photo by Nick Hillier on Unsplash

Did you ever get a shirt that was one size fits all? For some of us, it looked like a sleep shirt that was big and baggy. While others looked like a smedium.

JavaScript has only one number for us to use. So we don't have to learn multiple types as in Java or other languages. You can confuse yourself here.

JavaScript Number

So we can do things like this in JavaScript.

```
let num1 = 1.234;     // A number with decimals
let num2 = 5;         // A number without decimals
```

We can use decimals or we can use whole numbers.

```
let bigNum = 423e6;     // 423000000
let smallNum = 552e-5;   // 0.00552
```

When numbers get large we can use scientific notation too. These two show us how we can do that.

Number()

We can create with the number constructor too.

```
Number(999);
Number("999");
```

Both of these examples create a number. We can pass it a string or a number.

```
Number(true); // 1
Number(false); // 0
Number(new Date()); // 1712747922911
Number("sdfs:"); // NaN
```

In these examples, you can see that true and false resolve to numbers. The date is converted to one too. However, the letters do not resolve to a number. Therefore, it prints "NaN". This is for Not a Number, the reference guide shares more here.

Precision

JavaScript numbers are 64-bit floating-point. This follows the IEEE 754 standard. Integers are accurate to 15 places.

```
let num = 123456789012345;
```

The maximum number of decimals is 18.

```
let dec = 0.123456789012345678;
```

Methods

There are quite a few methods that JavaScript has for numbers. I will hit on a few here.

```
const num = Math.PI.toFixed(2);
console.log(num); // 3.14
```

The **toFixed** method will round a number to the decimal amount given. We are also using the Math.PI constant here as well. There are other Math constants detailed in the documentation.

```
const num = Math.PI.toPrecision(6);
console.log(num); // 3.14159
```

The toPrecision method will give us the numbers we ask for. So if you need to set how many significant digits display this will work for you.

There are a lot of options when working with JavaScript Numbers. Although they are a one-size-fits-all approach it works. Test out the limits when you work with them.

19

It Is Time To Spotlight the JavaScript Arrow Function

Photo by Nick Fewings on Unsplash

Programming requires us to learn as the technology changes.

JavaScript is no different. It has undergone large changes throughout the years. JavaScript Arrow functions are part of a major change that happened in 2015.

JavaScript Arrow Function

These are a concise substitute for functional expressions. They don't have the bindings for this, super, etc. Arrow functions can't be used as constructors either.

Arrow Functions are not original to JavaScript. This change was brought in part of ES6. This was a major change in the language.

Just as an example of what was done before arrow functions, this first example is a function expression, unlike the function declaration that is second here.

```
// function expression
message = function() {
  return "A message from Tom";
}


// function declaration
function functionDeclaration() {
  // statements
};
```

In ES6 and beyond we can do the following.

```
message = () => {
  return "A message from Tom";
}
```

If only one statement returns a value, you can do this.

```
message = () => "A message from Tom";
```

We can remove the brackets and return the statement. That is a short function!

Pass Parameter

Here is an example where we pass a parameter to the arrow function.

```
const yearUntilRetirement = birthYear => {
  const age = 2024 - birthYear;
  const retirement = 65 - age;
  return retirement;
}

console.log(yearUntilRetirement(1985)); // 26
```

The argument is the value we pass into the function. In this case, it is 1985. Some people use parameters and arguments interchangeably although they are slightly different.

To summarize the three types of functions in this example we see them all.

```
// function expression
message = function() {
  return "A message from Tom";
}

// function declaration
```

```
function functionDeclaration() {
  // statements
};


// arrow function
message = () => "A message from Tom";
```

We discussed the arrow function in-depth here. Each of the three types of JavaScript functions has its pros and cons. You must weigh them and decide what works best for your use case.

20

Valuable JavaScript Strict Equality and Targeted Inequality for the Best Outcome

Photo by Markus Winkler on Unsplash

I have to admit that equality in JavaScript can be confusing. I didn't fully grasp the differences until I took the time to review them. Three equal signs look odd to me.

Let's clear it up for you too. First off we can review strict equality. Then move to strict inequality. Lastly, we can wrap this up with an example and discussion of strict vs loose.

Strict Equality

Here are four examples to paint a picture for you. Take a close look at example three. That one might confuse you. These four should help you see how it works.

```
console.log(1 === 1);
// Example 1: Expected output: true

console.log('hello' === 'hello');
// Example 2: Expected output: true

console.log('1' === 1);
// Example 3: Expected output: false

console.log(0 === false);
// Example 4: Expected output: false
```

The first two make sense. There's nothing strange there. The third one you need to look closely. The first one is a string and the second one is a number. Therefore, JavaScript will declare that false.

Strict Inequality

After looking at the examples for equality, these make sense. Like learning opposites in Kindergarten we see a pattern. Here are four more examples of code.

```javascript
console.log(1 !== 1);
// Example 1: Expected output: false

console.log('hello' !== 'hello');
//Example 2: Expected output: false

console.log('1' !== 1);
//Example 3: Expected output: true

console.log(0 !== false);
//Example 4: Expected output: true
```

The proof is in the pudding, as developers, we like to see the code. These examples show us what is happening. As you begin to use the strict operators test your code. Pay attention to the edge cases. You may have some bugs lurking.

Strict vs Loose

Finally, let's compare strict vs loose. With just three variables we can explore some key differences.

```javascript
const zero = 0;
const zeroObj = new String("0");
const zeroStr = "0";

console.log(zero === zeroObj); // false
```

```
console.log(zero == zeroObj); // true

console.log(zero === zeroStr); // false
console.log(zero == zeroStr); // true

console.log(zeroObj === zeroStr); // false
console.log(zeroObj == zeroStr); // true
```

We have zero as a number, a string, and an object. You can see the big differences between the two types of equality. For this reason, many developers suggest not to use loose equality. It can lead to some difficult bugs to diagnose.

As you work on JavaScript make sure you understand strict and loose equality. If you have questions, review this thorough explanation of strict and loose or regular equality. It pays to know I have made mistakes here and it is quite helpful.

21

The Truth About JavaScript Object Notation is Found

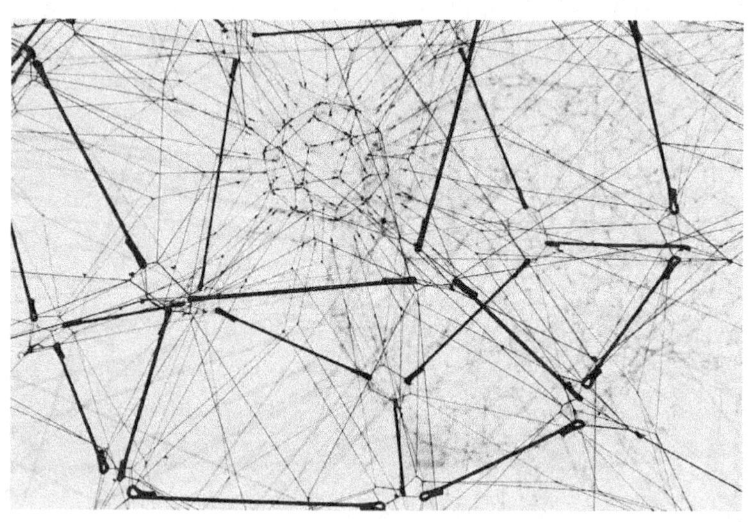

Photo by Alina Grubnyak on Unsplash

Developers are using data in almost everything we do. We

interact with many types of data, from a database or XML to JSON. JavaScript goes well together as that was the intention.

What is JSON?

According to JSON.org, they define it like this.

> **JSON** *(JavaScript Object Notation) is a lightweight data-interchange format. It is easy for humans to read and write. It is easy for machines to parse and generate.*

Where XML is more heavyweight and not quite human-readable JSON tries to reverse this. Of course, we can let you decide that. Here is an example.

```
'{"developer":"Tom", "linesOfCode": 12000,
"repo":"accounting", "ide": null}'
```

This object has a few properties. Developer, lines of code, repo, and ide. The basic structure is of keys and values. We could do the following if we want to access these properties in JavaScript.

```
let developer = obj.developer;
let linesOfCode = obj.linesOfCode;
let repository = obj.repo;
```

Here we can access the properties in the object easily with JavaScript. We have covered the basics let's compare JSON to XML.

JSON vs XML

These two types of data can be used in a lot of spaces. If we look at some similar examples we can compare them head to head. We can create an array of customers in both.

```
{"customers":[
  { "business":"ABC Inc.", "city":"Ducktown" },
  { "business":"Delta LTD", "city":"Jimmyville" },
  { "business":"XYZ Company", "city":"New Heights" }
]}
<customers>
  <customer>
    <business>ABC Inc.</business>
    <city>Ducktown</city>
  </customer>
  <customer>
    <business>Delta LTD</business>
    <city>Jimmyville</city>
  </customer>
  <customer>
    <business>XYZ Company</business> <city>New
    Heights</city>
  </customer>
</customers>
```

The tags in XML can make things longer. JSON makes things a little shorter too. Most programming languages can handle either one with the proper library.

Uses

JSON is used primarily to represent data for calling an API. Many developers prefer it over XML as it is lightweight. Also, it is language-independent so you can use it with most languages.

Here is an example of calling an API with JSON.

```
[
    {"command" : "ServerInfoService.getVersion"},
    {"command" : "Examples.echo","args" : {"echo" :
    "Some text."}}
]
```

The service may respond with this response.

```
[ {
    "result" : {
        "version" : "9.0.9000"
    }
}, {
    "result" : {
        "echo" : "Some text."
    }
} ]
```

Our friends at SmartBear detail this more in-depth here. This simple example gives you a basic understanding of calling an API or web service.

Working with JavaScript you will encounter JSON. This lightweight data format is easy to use. It has some distinct advantages over XML. Where at one time AJAX was more common today most web applications use JSON instead.

22

The Peril of JavaScript spread and Awesome Rest operator

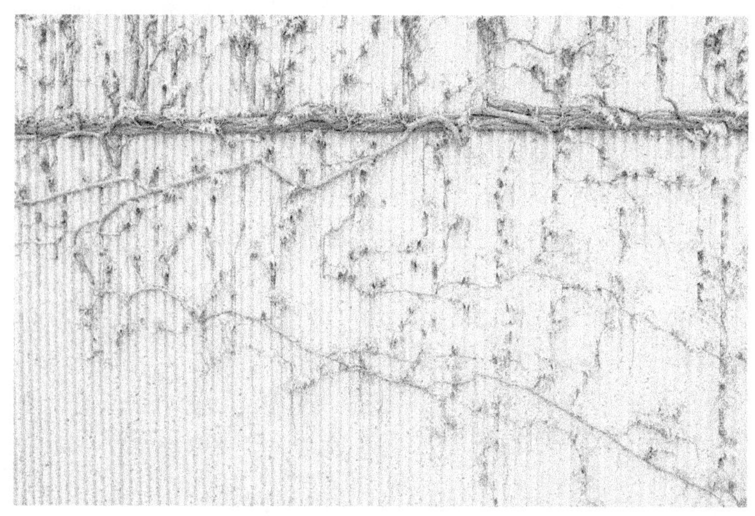

Photo by Scott Webb on Unsplash

As a kid, I would take things apart. My wristwatch, a radio, anything that I could get my hands on. I am still curious about how things work. Although, I try not to break things anymore.

Russian nesting dolls can be challenging. Each new one has another inside. JavaScript has something similar. The spread operator can help us break apart an array or string.

Spread Operator

The spread operator in JavaScript is (...) and is used to allow an array to be expanded into separate elements.

```
let numbers = [1,2,3,4,5];
let maximum = Math.max(...numbers);
let minimum = Math.min(...numbers);
console.log(maximum); // 5
console.log(minimum); // 1
```

Here we use it along with the Math operators to get the maximum and minimum of the array. This is only one handy use of the spread operator.

```
const policeSongs = ["King of Pain", "Wrapped Around
Your Finger"];
const stingSongs = ["Fields of Gold", ...policeSongs,
"Desert Rose"];
console.log(stingSongs); //  ["Fields of Gold","King
of Pain", "Wrapped Around Your Finger", "Desert Rose"]
```

If you need to mix arrays the spread operator can also do that. This can come in handy as you modify and add elements to arrays.

Rest Operator

The rest operator allows a function to handle different configurations of parameters. It can help set up an array or restructure an object.

```javascript
function total(...num) {
  let tot = 0;
  for (const n of numbers) {
    tot += n;
  }
  return tot;
}


console.log (total(11, 22, 33, 44)); // 110
```

This total function can handle multiple parameters passed to it. The rest operator enables that option.

Object Destructuring

If you have an array you might need to unpack the parts. To do this you can use object restructuring.

```javascript
const atariGames = ['Pitfall', 'Space Invaders',
'E.T.'];

const [great, good, awful] = atariGames;
```

This assigns each one of the three Atari games to an individual object. If necessary you can omit one and leave it empty like this.

```
const atariGames = ['Pitfall', 'Space Invaders',
'E.T.'];

const [great, , awful] = atariGames;
```

In this scenario, we only use the first and last games.

JavaScript gives you a lot of tools to handle arrays. The spread and rest operator can do some slicing and dicing. Then you can use object destructing to pull things apart. If you know your tools you can do about anything you want.

About the Author

Tom Henricksen is a problem-solving technology professional. He is a speaker and writer at Code is Easy. Starting from a developer he has worked as a Project Manager, Technical Lead, Scrum Master, and Manager of Software Development.

Tom has helped organizations with agile transformations. He has also coached and trained teams and individuals.

Tom has been an entrepreneur as well. He speaks and writes with a focus on technology roles. Tom was the founder of the Agile Online Summit and DevOps Online Summit where he led a strong online community of over 5,000 people.

Tom has learned how to solve challenging issues in technology and lead technical teams. He can help you develop those skills too!

You can connect with me on:

🌐 http://codeiseasy.co

🐦 https://x.com/TomHenricksen

🔗 https://www.linkedin.com/in/tomhenricksen

Subscribe to my newsletter:

✉ https://t.co/NkolrQgXHM